AF270425

Volcanic Eruptions

by Julie Murray

Level 1 – Beginning
Short and simple sentences with familiar words or patterns for children who are beginning to understand how letters and sounds go together.

Level 2 – Emerging
Longer words and sentences with more complex language patterns for readers who are practicing common words and letter sounds.

Level 3 – Transitional
More developed language and vocabulary for readers who are becoming more independent.

abdobooks.com

Published by Abdo Zoom, a division of ABDO, PO Box 398166, Minneapolis, Minnesota 55439. Copyright © 2025 by Abdo Consulting Group, Inc. International copyrights reserved in all countries. No part of this book may be reproduced in any form without written permission from the publisher. Dash!™ is a trademark and logo of Abdo Zoom.

Printed in the United States of America, North Mankato, Minnesota.
052024
092024

Photo Credits: Getty Images, Shutterstock
Production Contributors: Kenny Abdo, Jennie Forsberg, Grace Hansen, John Hansen
Design Contributors: Candice Keimig, Neil Klinepier

Library of Congress Control Number: 2023948528

Publisher's Cataloging in Publication Data

Names: Murray, Julie, author.
Title: Volcanic eruptions / by Julie Murray
Description: Minneapolis, Minnesota : Abdo Zoom, 2025 | Series: Natural disasters | Includes online resources and index.
Identifiers: ISBN 9781098285531 (lib. bdg.) | ISBN 9781098286231 (ebook) | ISBN 9781098286583 (Read-to-me eBook)
Subjects: LCSH: Natural disasters--Juvenile literature. | Volcanic eruptions--Juvenile literature. | Geoscience (Geology)--Juvenile literature. | Volcanology--Juvenile literature. | Geodynamics-Juvenile literature.
Classification: DDC 904.5--dc23

Table of Contents

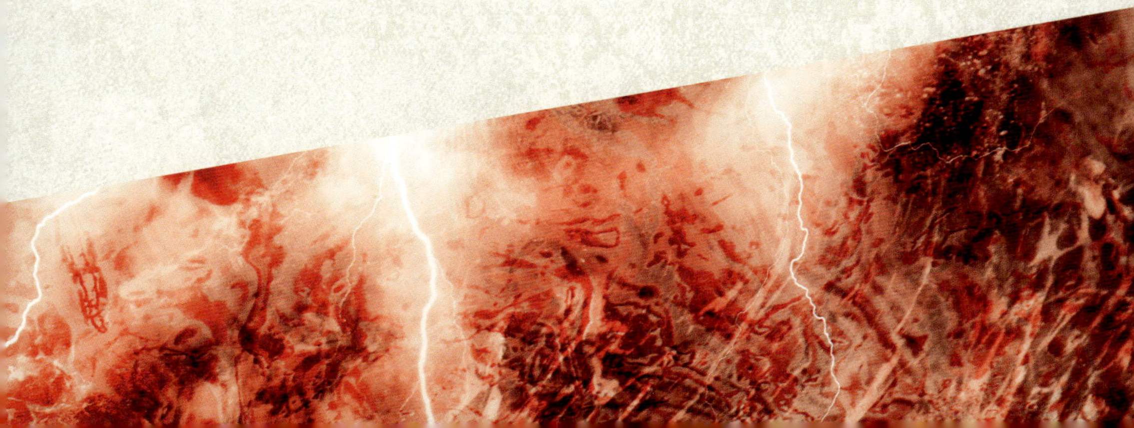

Volcanic Eruptions

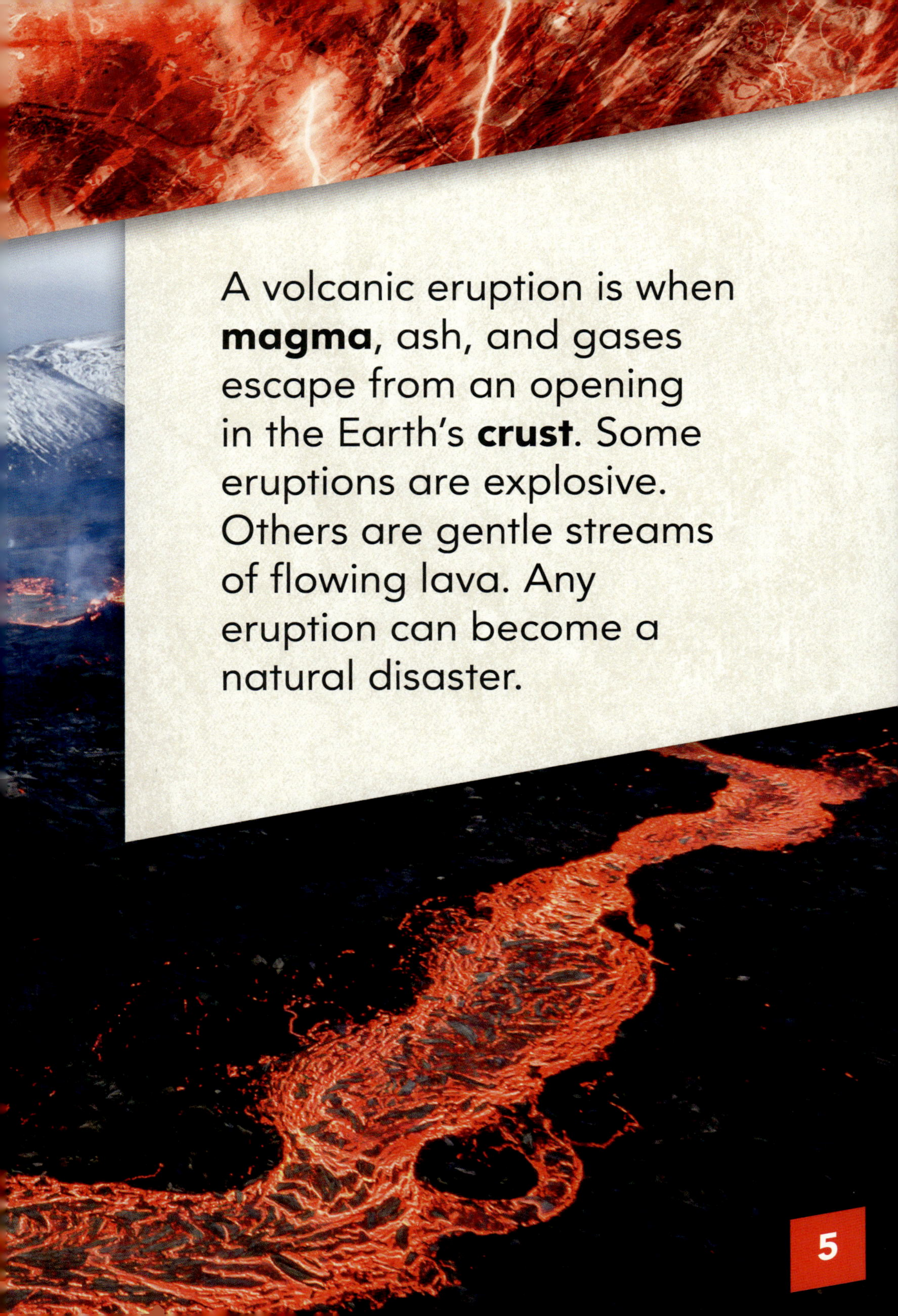

A volcanic eruption is when **magma**, ash, and gases escape from an opening in the Earth's **crust**. Some eruptions are explosive. Others are gentle streams of flowing lava. Any eruption can become a natural disaster.

Causes

Earth's outer **crust** is made up of **plates**. They fit together like puzzle pieces. The Ring of Fire is a meeting point for many of these plates. About 75% of Earth's volcanoes are found here.

Plates move and collide. This creates **pressure** deep in the Earth. It is so hot there that rock melts into **magma**. This pressure pushes magma up to the surface.

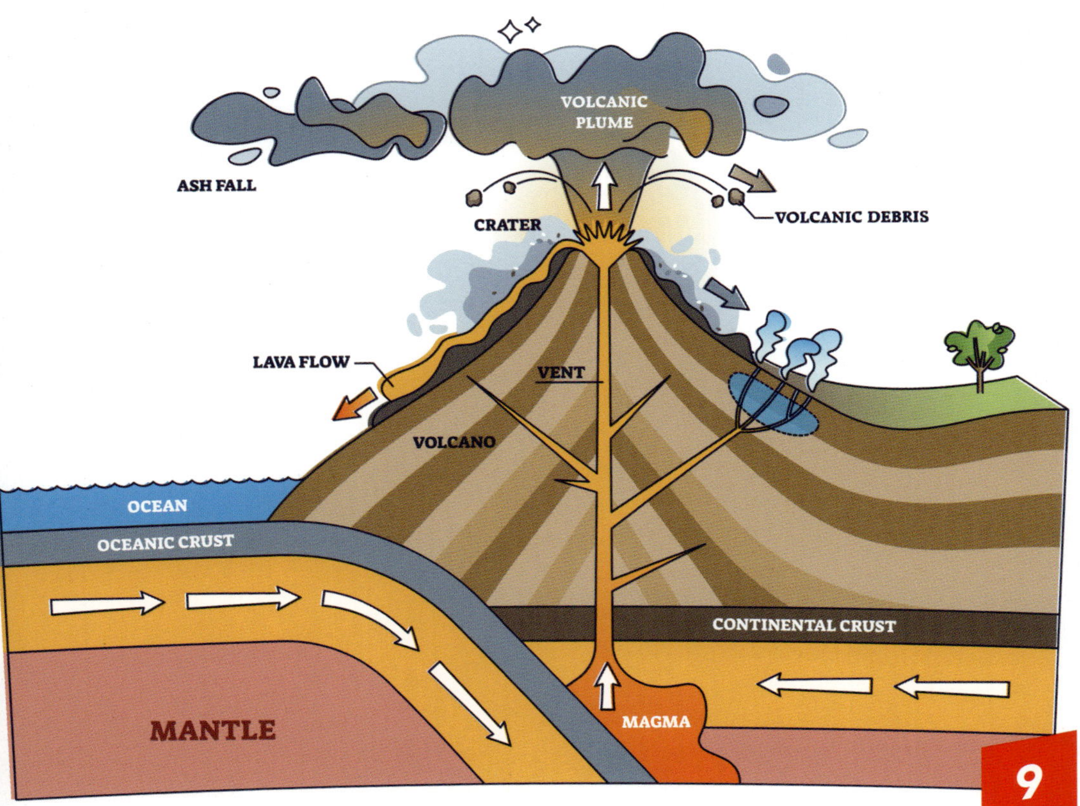

As the **magma** moves, gases build up. The **pressure** increases. The magma looks for ways to escape. Runny magma escapes through cracks. Thick magma gets trapped. This causes an explosive eruption.

Once **magma** reaches the surface it is called lava. After an eruption, ash and lava cool and harden forming new rock.

Over time, volcanoes can grow bigger and bigger. Their shapes are constantly changing.

Effects

Volcanic eruptions can send rock, lava, and gases high into the air. **Volcanic plumes** can reach heights of more than 145,000 feet (44,196 m). This is almost 28 miles (45.1 km) high!

Falling **debris** and ash can cause major problems. Ash clouds fill the sky. This creates poor air quality. Ash can cover cities and crops. It can also contaminate water sources.

Lava reaches temperatures up to 2,200° F (1,200° C). Flowing lava destroys everything in its path. It can also spark fires along the way. The lava can spread out over many miles!

18

19

Eruptions can destroy entire cities. Mount Vesuvius erupted in 79 CE. It buried the city of Pompeii and its people under 20 feet (6.1 m) of ash and **debris**. It remained that way for thousands of years. Today, much of the city has been uncovered.

- More than 80% of the Earth's surface was formed by volcanic activity.

- There are more than 1,500 active volcanoes around the world. Mauna Lao is the largest one. It is on the Big Island in Hawaii.

- Volcanic eruptions can cause other natural disasters. Landslides, tsunamis, and wildfires can all be **triggered** by an eruption.

Glossary

crust – the outer layer of Earth.

debris – scattered pieces left after something has been destroyed.

magma – hot, liquid matter beneath the earth's surface that cools to form igneous rock.

plate – a tectonic plate, one of the parts of the outer layer of planet Earth.

pressure – a steady force upon a surface.

triggered – caused by a particular situation.

volcanic plume – a mixture of hot volcanic particles, water vapor, gases and air put into the air after an explosive eruption.

Index

Online Resources

Booklinks
NONFICTION NETWORK
FREE! ONLINE NONFICTION RESOURCES

To learn more about Volcanic Eruptions, please visit **abdobooklinks.com** or scan this QR code. These links are routinely monitored and updated to provide the most current information available.